GRANDMOTHER TREE

The Song of the Forests

Kate Norris

NATIONAL LIBRARY OF AUSTRALIA

A catalogue record for this book is available from the National Library of Australia

ISBN: 978-0-6486813-04 (paperback).

Publishing Details
Published in Australia – Shufflewing Publications

Publishing Consultants
Cover and Interior Layout: Pickawoowoo Publishing Group

Printed & Channel Distribution
Lightning Source / Ingram

For all the forest spirits,
with a dedication to Warren,
with much love and gratitude.

One fine Sunday morning Sophie's parents took her to the forest for a picnic. They went to one of their favourite places, a sunny glade next to a bubbling stream. Tall Jarrah and Marri trees surrounded the clearing and brightly coloured wildflowers grew scattered throughout the grass. Birds fluttered busily amongst the trees and their calls and whistles made a pleasant background melody for the family's picnic.

After lunch Sophie's parents lay quietly reading and talking while Sophie explored the nearby forest. She scrambled and leapt over rocks, crept through blossom covered shrubs and peered into the clear running stream. Growing tired she curled up in the roots of a friendly looking Marri tree. The soothing hum of the bees high in the branches soon lulled her to sleep.

She dreamt ...

The old tree that Sophie slept beneath reached down a branch and gently tickled her with her leaves. Sophie opened her eyes and smiled up at the Grandmother tree as sunlight dappled her bark and her leaves rustled softly.

"Wake up, Sophie!" Grandmother Tree whispered, "It's time for a story."

Grandmother Tree then scooped Sophie up with one of her branches. Sophie laughed in delight as she scrambled along the limb to nestle into the fork of Grandmother Tree's trunk. She enjoyed the feel of her rough bark on her cheek as she leant against her. Looking down Sophie could see her parents still seated on the picnic rug in the distance.

"I'm ready, Grandmother Tree!" she said as she made herself comfortable, "What story do you have to tell me?"

Grandmother Tree's barked face became sad as she spoke softly, "We trees can speak to one another. Did you know that, Sophie?"

Sophie shook her head as Grandmother Tree continued, "When I was young, I could hear the voices of so many of us, a great song that I was part of. Every tree voice raised in harmony, all passing our tales from one to another. As time has passed so many of those voices have stopped singing. Now I hear so few of us and those I do hear are getting fainter and fainter. I miss hearing my brothers and sisters."

Sophie could sense the tree's sadness.

"Why can't you hear the other trees anymore?" she asked Grandmother Tree.

Softly brushing Sophie's hair with her leaves, Grandmother Tree replied, "There are not so many of us left anymore. People have cut us down to make space for their houses and roads. They have used our timber to make buildings, furniture and paper. Where vast forests once stood, now lay barren landscapes destroyed by your farming and mining practices. However, that's not why I'm telling you this story. If you look out upon this forest you will see many trees and plants that still dwell here. I want to tell you about a new danger that we now face."

Sophie gazed out over the many forest trees, the stately Jarrahs and Marris, the graceful Peppermints and bright Wattles. She imagined them all singing and talking to each other and wondered what else could be threatening these peaceful beings.

Grandmother Tree's soft voice continued, "Many of us are growing sick now. It's becoming harder and harder to hear each other because the air is so polluted with the noise and frequency that comes from your technology. There's an artificial signal that is given out by your mobile phones and their towers, by your computers and internet. It blocks our song and hurts us.

Our little ones struggle to grow and our elders are weak and prone to disease. This unnatural frequency harms all living things, including humans, though you do not sense it. It affects the bees and other insects which are so important for the health of the forests. They are needed to pollinate our flowers so we can grow the seeds that become our young ones. Now the bees are becoming confused and sick as well."

Sophie looked out over the forest in despair, wondering about how much people affected everything around them without realising it.

"What can I do to make a difference?" she asked Grandmother Tree.

"You can share our story," the old tree replied, "Tell your family and friends about us. Ask them to turn off their mobile phones when they come to visit. Tell them, if they come and they are quiet, if they turn off their loud cars and music and if they stop always talking over the top of each other, then they might just hear us sing. Tell them if they are quiet and still, if they come with respect in their hearts, they may see all the other things that live amongst us."

As Grandmother Tree spoke, she ruffled her leaves making Sophie look upwards. Sophie gasped as she realised that many types of animals and beings were hidden amongst Grandmother Tree's branches. Small marsupials scampered past and a possum peeked shyly from its hollow in the trunk. Butterflies, bees and dragonflies danced amongst the leaves while an assortment of birds wove between the branches. From the corner of her eye, Sophie caught the flicker of wings and realised in amazement that nature spirits playfully flittered around her. She could hear their faint laughter amid the rustle of the leaves.

"There's so much living within the forests that people cannot see," Grandmother Tree murmured, "That is because they have forgotten how to look. They are too distracted by their phones and their own loud voices. They miss out on so much."

Sophie sat quietly, awed by all the secret life that surrounded her. She wondered about what else people missed out on experiencing because they were always so busy and noisy.

Eventually Grandmother Tree gently jostled Sophie to catch her attention again.

"It's time to go back now," the tree said as she reached up a branch.

Sophie stepped onto the branch and Grandmother Tree lowered her carefully to the ground. Drowsiness overcame Sophie as she made her way back to where she had first fallen asleep. Comfortably nestled into the curved roots again she heard Grandmother Tree speak, "Remember to come back to visit us, Sophie. You are always welcome here."

"Thank you, Grandmother Tree, I definitely will," Sophie mumbled in reply.

She closed her eyes and drifted back into the darkness of sleep. Faintly, she could hear her name being called through the stillness.

She woke...

Opening her eyes sleepily, Sophie could see her mum waving to her from the picnic rug.

"Time to go home, Soph," her mum called to her.

As Sophie stood up, she looked up into the branches of the tree that she had been sleeping beneath. The breeze rustled the leaves in a gently murmured song. Birds cheerfully darted through the branches while insects hurried about their business. The flash of a furred tail and glint of friendly dark eyes revealed a possum as it curled up in its cosy hollow. Shimmers of light amongst the leaves caught Sophie's eye and made her wonder if it was the wings of nature spirits as they frolicked throughout the branches. Smiling, she patted the tree's rough bark then turned to make her way back to her parents.

Back at the picnic rug, Sophie's mum was packing away the remains of lunch while her dad was busy on his mobile phone. Sitting down next to him, Sophie gently took the phone from his hands and turned it off.

"Soph!" her dad reproached her, "I was halfway through doing something."

"Not here, Dad," Sophie said to him, "It's not good for the trees."

Her dad raised his eyebrows at her questioningly and asked, "What do you mean?"

"Your phone signal hurts all the trees, animals and people within its range," Sophie replied to him.

Both Sophie's parents paused to look at her.

"How do you know that, Soph?" her dad asked.

"A tree told me, Dad," Sophie smiled at him, "Did you know that trees talk to each other? I can tell you all about it."

Sophie's mum laughed as she stood up with the picnic basket.

"That sounds like a very interesting story," she said, "Come on you two, let's head home and Sophie can tell us what she has learnt on the way."

As Sophie walked back to the car with her parents, she told them about the forests and how mobile phones and Wi-Fi signals affected them. She spoke to them about all the things she saw living in the treetops and how the trees were sad that they could no longer share their songs. She explained that all the forests and their inhabitants were becoming sick while people didn't even notice or realise that they were the ones causing it.

Before reaching the car to return home Sophie paused in her story to glance back towards the forest. Standing tall amongst the other forest trees she could see Grandmother Tree; her barked face was creased into a peaceful smile as she gracefully waved a branch at Sophie in farewell.